THE
BLUFFER'S GUIDE®
TO
BALLET

CRAIG DODD

D1635733

Oval Books

Published by Oval Books
335 Kennington Road
London SE11 4QE
United Kingdom

Telephone: +44 (0)20 7582 7123
Fax: +44 (0)20 7582 1022
E-mail: info@ovalbooks.com
Web site: www.ovalbooks.com

First published by Ravette Publishing, 1988
Reprinted/updated: 1991,1993

First published by Oval Books, 2002
Updated 2003

Series Editor – Anne Tauté

Cover designer – Jim Wire, Quantum
Printer – Cox & Wyman Ltd
Producer – Oval Projects Ltd

The Bluffer's Guides® series is based
on an original idea by Peter Wolfe.

The Bluffer's Guide®, The Bluffer's Guides®,
Bluffer's®, and Bluff Your Way® are
Registered Trademarks.

In the highly unlikely event of any
faux pas the author will make suitable
amendations in future editions,
avec révérence.

ISBN: 1-903096-26-X

CONTENTS

WHAT BALLET IS

Ballet is simply formalised dancing, evolved over four centuries from court dance. It now bears roughly the sort of relationship to its origins that Fred Astaire and Ginger Rogers do to ballroom dancing. Precious little.

Its terminology is French, coming from court dance and horse ballets. Its most obvious special feature is that ballerinas perform the totally unnatural feat of dancing on the tips of their toes. This is called dancing *en pointe*. As a result ballerinas' feet are not a pretty sight, and give chiropodists a field day.

Ballet roughly divides into three compartments.

1. **Classical** – The purest form, based on the grand Russian style of the 19th century, though the French may have views on this. It is seen at its purest in the great classic ballets such as *Swan Lake* or *The Sleeping Beauty*.

2. **Neo-classical** – Very much identified with the work of choreographer Balanchine starting in the late 1920s when he transformed his classical training at the Imperial Ballet of the Tsar into a personal style, in ballets such as *Apollo*. He went on to create many other plotless pure-dance works. In recent years neo-classicism has often come to mean old ballets in new leotards.

3. **Modern Ballet** – Simply the classical vocabulary of steps distorted in any way to express what a particular choreographer wants. This can encompass the sexual contortions of Béjart, the athleticism of Kylian or the jazz inspired works of Alvin Ailey, but is not to be confused with modern dance which is a different kettle of *poisson* and not within the scope of this definitive volume.

How to Enjoy Ballet

The best advice to offer anyone with a mental block about ballet is that they should just sit back and enjoy it. Thinking at the ballet is not to be encouraged. The most frequent complaint heard about ballet is "I don't know what it means", said by people with the mistaken belief that anyone actually involved in the business does.

Ballet has been described as a dangerous art, very seductive and liable to arouse previously hidden emotions. It must be faced, ballet is a physical business and, to put it bluntly, sexual. Anyone who pretends they like a particular dancer purely for their arabesque is talking tosh. Looks come into it too, and those who say otherwise are being economical with the truth. A pretty face (on either sex) can make up for lots of technical faults. A brilliant technician, if less than moderately good looking, may have to battle the way to the top.

Mime

Mime can be the great hang-up for the beginner and is yet another reason for people to complain that they don't understand ballet. This is hard to credit as ballet mime is so simple-minded it makes charades seem like brain surgery. For instance:

a) If the Princess Mother in *Swan Lake* points to her ring finger you can safely guess she's telling Siegfried it's time to wed and not admiring her nail polish. The same goes for Aurora in *The Sleeping Beauty* who quite clearly has four princes waiting to woo her.

6

b) Hands swirled above the head, like mixing pastry, means dance. Admittedly this may not be immediately obvious, but as dancing invariably takes place thereafter it is not a matter of immediate concern.

c) Hands placed on the chest indicate love, not indigestion. A raised arm giving a two-finger salute (fingers together, boy-scout fashion) swears that the love will be eternal. Experienced bluffers will know that this means some serious two-timing is in the offing.

In one or two of the big story ballets there are longer passages of mime which no-one really understands without a programme note. On first viewing you should not feel left out if you do not realise that the Swan Queen is explaining that the lake is made from her mothers' tears or that Giselle's mother is telling the yokels that the local woods are haunted by the spirits of girls who died after being jilted. It will not spoil your overall enjoyment of the ballet to have a brief nap while this is going on. It's all in the music anyway.

Name-calling

It is essential to be aware of the right mode of address when discussing people in the ballet. The correct use of dancers' and choreographers' names can suggest greater knowledge of the ballet world; indeed, even intimacy with some of its inhabitants.

Dancers tend to be called by their Christian names. Diminutives are used rarely, unless the dancer is Russian, when it is almost obligatory, Mikhail Baryshnikov (Misha), Dimitri Gruzdyev (Dima), etc. Choreographers or directors are invariably called by their surnames, Neumeier, Martins, Forsythe, and so on. Not John, Peter, or Billy. Thus if you were, for instance, enthusing about a performance by Royal Ballet star Alina Cojacaru you might say "Wasn't Alina fabulous tonight?", which is just as well as no-one can pronounce 'Cojacaru'.

The assiduous ballet bluffer will soon pick up the names in common usage. There are a few exceptions, usually involving the all-time greats who have become much-loved fixtures and fittings of the ballet world. An Ashton ballet may be announced, but you should refer to it as one by "Sir Fred". And Balanchine may have been an institution, but "Mr. B." did the daily work; Dame Ninette de Valois created the Royal Ballet but "Madam" ran it for over 30 years.

In at least one area of ballet, life has become easier for the bluffer. The use of camp backstage names has waned. A whole generation of Dorises, Monas and Hetties, even a Joan of Archives (company historian), are now distinguished gentlemen, teaching or directing.

Who's Who

The ballet world is inhabited by a curious set of deeply interdependent people. Some are actively involved, others strictly on the sidelines. Here are a few tips on how to spot them. Insiders include:

The Artistic Director

The Artistic Director is usually a choreographer or dancer either retired or, quite often these days, still dancing. More often than not they are budding mega-lomaniacs who listen to no-one, ruining careers at whim,

8

often under the mistaken belief they are helping them.

Bluffers should remember that the greatest artistic director was Diaghilev who did not choreograph, dance, design or compose. Nowadays companies cannot afford this luxury and actually expect some work from the director. Other than acting like a god, they usually create ballets or, if they are still dancing, hog the best rôles for themselves.

The Choreographer

These are the men and women who make the ballets; not just the steps, but the whole production. With varying degrees of success they choose the story, the music and the designer. Between nervous breakdowns and creative crises they spend most of their time trying to convince everyone except themselves that they know what they are doing.

They are the most important people in the company as everyone else from the dancers to the stage staff, designers and ultimately the administrative staff, depend upon their creativity. All, that is, except the musicians, who have such a stranglehold on the theatre that even if there is no work they can still turn up and get paid.

The Music Director/Conductor

The conductor has the thankless task of trying to get a passable result out of the musicians. They in turn have the thankless task of playing a lot of ballet music which, musically speaking, can leave a lot to be desired. The conductor should have some rapport with the dancers, but often he buries his head in the score and ignores what is happening on the stage.

Great conductors who demean themselves with the

9

occasional ballet performance will all too often play at their own tempo, usually more suited to a concert performance, leaving the dancers to cope as best they can. If it doesn't look good, the dancer gets the blame and the conductor gets the good reviews.

Orchestral playing for ballet very often leaves room for improvement, which is not always the fault of the conductor. In opera house companies it has been known for the conductor to have a good rehearsal with the orchestra in the morning, only to turn up for the evening performance and hardly recognise a face in the orchestra pit. For reasons losts in the mists of time and union negotiations, musicians are allowed to nominate deputies if they have something better to do. Why this is allowed to happen is a major mystery of the ballet world.

The Pianist

This is the person who plays for the daily ballet class, as well as rehearsals. They have to possess the patience of Job to play fairly nondescript music for class and then spend the rest of the day endlessly repeating phrases of music for rehearsals. On top of that, they have to cope with the whims of dancers and choreographers, which led one pianist to cry "How do you want it today. Too slow or too fast?"

The Ballet Master/Mistress

The person who really runs the ballet company day-by-day, this post is often held by a dancer put out to grass and who is therefore in a position to settle old scores by influencing the casting of rôles, usually to the benefit of his or her (temporary) favourites. Supervising endless rehearsals and teaching dancers new rôles takes infinite patience, an eagle eye and endless packets of cigarettes.

The Notators

These people write down the ballets in strange hieroglyphics on music paper. The most widely-used system is called choreology, invented by Joan and Rudolf Benesh. It's so widely-used that notators are invariably called choreologists. They are the guardians of the holy writ, the bible in which ballets are written down and which is consulted during rehearsals.

The Dancers

If bluffers mingle with dancers they will soon find that there is only one topic of conversation – other dancers. It's best not to try to bluff your way with a dancer as they have invariably lived and breathed ballet from a very early age and rarely know nor care about anything else. There is little you can say to impress a dancer other than to offer to buy dinner.

Fortunately dancers can be spotted a mile off by their turned-out feet and the inevitable dance bag slung over their shoulder – invariably Gucci or Louis Vuitton, even for the lowliest member of the corps de ballet. Or an exotic back-pack.

All are striking to look at no matter how genuinely good or bad looking they are. They all know how to wear clothes with effect. Though most can make the contents of an Oxfam shop look the height of fashion they tend to be members of the Designer Tendency, with special interest in the leather and suede departments. Conservationists fear for the lives of herds of animals which have to be slaughtered annually to dress leading dancers.

Surprisingly many dancers smoke. Marlboro is the brand leader and they smoke them by the packet. Though some companies have declared studios smoke free zones they seem to have had little effect on total consumption. Ashtrays make a convenient missile for choreographers to heave around at trying moments.

Life in a ballet company is very incestuous with dancers having affairs or marrying each other in infinite combinations. A few form relationships outside the ballet world, but the nature of ballet life, rehearsing together all day and performing together every evening, makes this difficult. A few spectacular break-outs over the years have included marriages to a Sainsbury, a Marquess and a clutch of merchant bankers. Two Royal Ballet ballerinas have even been married to ballet critics.

Dancers live in an hierarchical world, i.e:

1. At the top of the pile is that rare creature, the **prima ballerina assoluta**, only one or two a lifetime, which can be quite enough. Some like **Margot Fonteyn** were charm itself, but others like **Sylvie Guillem** ('Madam Non!') seem to have read far more into the title than was ever intended. The male equivalent doesn't technically exist, but several dancers seem to think it does to judge by their off-stage behaviour.

2. The next category down is the plain **ballerina** or **principal dancer**, those who really head companies and dance the lion's share of the major rôles.

3. Waiting in the wings and eager to share those rôles are the **soloists** who do even more work, as they must be able to step in for an indisposed principal or corps de ballet member.

4. Below the soloists come the **coryphées**, a term which in translation from the Greek can mean either a

leading dancer in a ballet or a chorus member. This aptly defines the no-man's land they inhabit having graduated from the corps de ballet, but not quite made it to soloists. Dancers can languish in this limbo for years.

5. At the bottom of the pile are the unsung heroes and heroines of the ballet, the **corps de ballet**. They are destined to appear in almost every ballet grasping at any tiny opportunity to shine and catch a choreographer's eye. But all too often they are left standing around as human scenery with fixed smiles on their faces trying to convince themselves and the audience that their years of expensive and dedicated training are being put to good use.

The Real VIPs

While the inward-looking ballet world dances in ever decreasing circles, the really important people devotedly buy tickets (except for critics who get them for nothing) at ever increasing prices. These long-suffering outsiders include:

Balletomanes

Not all ballet lovers are balletomanes. As the title implies these are the dedicated groupies of the dance world for whom dance is the world. Trying to bluff your way with a balletomane is a fool venture as they know everything, particularly about their favourite dancers. They know all the current gossip about ballet personalities and politics and, if over a certain age, are sure to have seen **Ulanova** dance *Giselle* in 1956 and hanker after a golden age of ballet when all dancers were greater artistes than those on the stage today. Should you accidentally fall into conversation with a balletomane make some quick excuse to get yourself to the other end of the bar as soon as possible.

The main function of a true balletomane is to massage the ego of dancers by sending cards and small presents on opening nights and wait outside stage doors in all weathers to present flowers or collect autographs.

Ballet Mothers

Ballet mothers are not recognised by any outward feature, but only by the glazed look on the eyes of those to whom they are talking. They are invariably singing the praises of their talented offspring and lamenting how artistic directors just do not seem to appreciate that talent. In fact they do, all too well, which is why they insist on casting the talented offspring as one of Juliet's friends, while Juliet is danced by some truly talented 16-year-old.

On no account humour a ballet mother out of kindness as this will guarantee that the next time your paths cross she will bear straight down on you, certain of a fair, unbiased, hearing. Escape to the other end of the bar is not advised in this case as she is sure to follow. Simply wave at some mythical friend in the crowd and disappear into it. The original ballet mum was probably Catherine de Medici (see Terrine de Ballet).

Critics

Those who review ballet performances for the national and provincial press speak a language of their own, largely for their own benefit or for the hordes of dancers who swear they never read reviews.

Critics usually sit in aisle seats to effect hasty exits

at the end of performances, ostensibly to get their copy in quickly, but in practice merely to get to the free interval drinks or to the bar ahead of anyone else. It can be educational to eavesdrop in the bar and hear the truly bitchy comments which are said about performances, but never appear in print.

How to Translate a Ballet Review

Remember that critics hunt in packs. Careful reading, usually between the lines, will reveal pack leaders and camp followers. You will soon learn to recognise that if the *Daily Bugle* likes a performance, the *Daily Thunderer* is likely to approve as well. But, just as night follows day, the *Evening Crier* and the *Evening Bystander* will dislike it. Astute observation can therefore greatly reduce a ballet lover's newspaper bill. Look out for the following phrases.

Promising – Suggests much, but is rarely fulfilled. Many dancers remain promising until retirement.

Dependable – An over-30-year-old who was once promising.

Coped well with the technical demands – Fell over but is a long-time favourite of the critic.

Partnered strongly – Threw the ballerina round with excessive force.

Partnered tentatively – Dropped the ballerina.

Dazzling technique – Flashy steps at the expense of all else.

Sensitive artistry – Simpered excessively. The French and Italians excel at this.

Well-schooled – Dull.

Innovative choreography – Obscure or downright perverse.

Avant-garde choreography – Something supported by public subsidy entirely for the benefit of the choreographer involved.

Enfant terrible of ballet – Terribly childish choreographer.

Interesting interpretation – The critic hadn't a clue what the dancer was doing.

Let the rôle speak through the steps – The dancer couldn't act for toffee.

A triumph of acting ability – The dancer couldn't dance for toffee.

Made his/her presence felt – Upstaged everyone else.

Guest artiste – Either an expensive import, or the company humouring an old dancer doing a bit part.

Lively tempo – The orchestra managed to keep well ahead of the dancers.

Triple-bill – Three short ballets with two long intervals. The Royal Ballet are the market leaders in this department.

Gala evening – Odds and ends of ballets the company couldn't make a regular evening of.

Royal gala – As above, but at higher prices and graced by a minor royal.

Invaluable programme notes – The ballet was unintelligible. Or the critic wrote the synopsis.

TERRINE DE BALLET (Potted History)

The true ballet bluffer does not really need to know any ballet history at all. It is highly unlikely that in-depth historical analysis will take place even in such a temple of ballet worship as the amphitheatre of the Royal Opera House. Ballet is a *now* art, much concerned with current favourites and fancies, but a few salient facts might help if you are taken by a desperate urge to up-stage a persistent know-all (or fellow bluffer) or to understand the occasional historical reference by a critic with academic pretensions, of which there are too many.

Ballet at Court

Ballet, a mannered and fussy art form at the best of times, not surprisingly had its origins in the small courts of Italy in the early 16th century.

These court entertainments were taken to France in the middle of the century as part of the baggage of Catherine de Medici when she married Henri II. She employed **Beaujoyeux** as her dancing master to organise the great court entertainments arranged to divert her three sons while she ran the country.

Her greatest creation, and the only one you need know about, was the *Ballet Comique de la Reine* of 1573. But beware. These **ballet de cour** were not ballets as we know them today. They were spectacles lasting hours and involving soldiers marching in formation, exotic animals, singing, verse, horse ballets and, not least, food. They were more like the opening of the Sydney Olympics than a ballet.

Louis XIV, nicknamed the *Sun King* after his rôle at the centre of the *Ballet de la Nuit,* is the one who can be said to have put ballet on the world stage. From

17

his first dance steps at the age of 12 he became an accomplished dancer and his interest led him to create the **Royal Academy of Music** (1661) and the **Royal Academy of Dance** (1671) in Paris, to formalise steps and style. Over the centuries the Academy developed into the Paris Opéra of today.

At roughly the same time in Russia, Peter the Great promoted things French in the hope that they would civilise his courtiers. Russian costume was forbidden and dancing was introduced to court. From this, and the forming of an **Academy of Dance** by Empress Anna Ivanovna in 1738, grew the mighty court ballet of the Tsar. Ballet lovers generally consider this a good thing.

Bring on the Ballerina

The rise of the ballerina is in direct proportion to the rise of her hemline. Note that the first true ballerina was **Marie de Camargo** at the beginning of the 18th century, and that when she raised the hem of her hooped dress to show off her nifty footwork it was the first step in the upward rise of skirts and therefore, ballet. **Marie Sallé** wore revealing classical draperies in *Pygmalion* in the decadent London of 1734.

Dresses then shortened to the romantic tutu, the short classical tutu, painted body tights and eventually, in Nederlands Dans Theater's *Mutations*, vanished altogether.

Men on the Stage

By the middle of the 18th century, ballet was hampered with masks, singing, speech, cumbersome costumes, and stories restricted to kings and queens, gods and goddesses, nymphs and a few shepherds. **Jean**

Georges Noverre proposed some radical changes, and Dauberval got the message and choreographed *La Fille Mal Gardée*, the first story of everyday country folk. It has been running longer than *The Archers*.

The Italian **Salvatore Vigano** took up these ideas having established himself at La Scala in Milan after inheriting a fortune from an admirer. Dancers still hit lucky this way, and if they don't inherit fortunes, they often marry them. But it was one of his young colleagues, **Carlo Blasis,** who wrote the definitive guide to technique, *The Code of Terpsichore*. It is from his teaching that the present day classical vocabulary comes. He also devised the *attitude* pose.

Men had a bit of a come back in the late 18th century with **Gaetano Vestris** jumping higher than anyone else, earning the title 'God of the Dance'. His son **Auguste**, took over the title and was still able to partner the young **Marie Taglioni**, when he was 75.

The Romantic Era

Marie Taglioni ushered in the new age, performing what is regarded as the first ballet to incorporate the elements of romanticism, handy for any bluffer to know, in the opera *Robert the Devil* by Meyerbeer, in which as the Abbess she led ghostly nuns around a moonlit cloister Her father, **Filippo**, created *La Sylphide* for her, and soon stages were overrun by sylphs, wilis and naiads (see Glossary) in exotic places like Scotland, though you should realise that to judge from the shoes of the period ballerinas did not stay on their toes for long.

Taglioni's greatest rival was the fiery and temperamental **Fanny Elssler**, famous for her Spanish dance *Cachucha*, and the first Romantic ballerina to visit America where she stayed too long and was fired by the Paris Opéra. The era also produced **Carlotta Grisi**, who was the first Ondine, and **Lucille Grahn**, for whom **Bournonville** created his version of *La Sylphide*. These three ballerinas joined Taglioni in London in 1845 for the last great performance of the Romantic era, the famous *Pas de Quatre*.

Coping with four mega-stars was almost too much for Benjamin Lumley, manager of Her Majesty's Theatre where the event was staged. Faced with the problem of who should appear top of the bill Lumley simply said "Let the oldest have the honour".

Russian Revolt

When French dancer **Marius Petipa** arrived in Russia, the Imperial Ballet was constructed just like the court, culminating with **Kshessinska**, the absolute prima ballerina assoluta, who wore real jewellery for performances. Mere prima ballerinas included the Italians, **Virginia Zucchi**, **Pierina Legnani**, the first Swan Queen, and **Carlotta Brianza**, the first Aurora. (Note that when *The Sleeping Beauty* was revived almost 50 years later she mimed the rôle of the bad fairy.)

The revolt against the rigid Imperial Ballet was first expressed in articles in *Mir Isskusstva* (The World of Art) by **Serge Diaghilev**, the painter **Leon Bakst**, and the designer **Alexander Benois** (who once cooked and ate one of Taglioni's pointe shoes). Diaghilev had ideal qualifications for an artistic director: he didn't dance, compose, design or choreograph.

By 1909 his Ballet Russe was mounting seasons in Paris with such works as *Scheherezade*, *Prince Igor*, *The Firebird* and *Petrouchka*. Equally important, he introduced the very modern (for the time) music of **Stravinsky**, the striking designs of painters such as

Gontcharova, the dancing of **Anna Pavlova** (the greatest ballerina of the age), and the oriental-looking sensation, **Vaslav Nijinsky**.

Nijinskymania

Born in 1888, Nijinsky became involved with Diaghilev (like father and son is the usual euphemism) and joined him in Paris after being dismissed from the Imperial Ballet for not wearing the obligatory extra shorts over his tights. There he astounded audiences with his dancing and choreography until marriage to **Romola Pulsky** led Diaghilev to dispense with his services.

He gave his last performance as Petrouchka in 1917 and spent over 30 years in mental homes before dying in 1950 in London where he was buried – until **Serge Lifar,** another Diaghilev protégé, had Nijinsky's body removed to Paris so that he could be buried alongside it. (Such ego).

Cocktail Time

Having produced a stream of great ballets in the 1920s, Diaghilev found himself, in his own words 'a bartender mixing cocktails'. He tried every sort of exotic brew: Nijinska's smart ballets, Balanchine's early experiments such as *La Chatte*, and Jean Cocteau-inspired concoctions. The effort exhausted him. A prediction that he would die on water had kept him at home when Nijinsky sailed off to South America and marriage. Ironically, in 1929, he died on holiday in Venice.

You can make much of the fact that while Diaghilev changed the face of ballet during his life, it was his death (and thus the break-up of his company) that scattered dancers worldwide, producing the seeds from which today's mega-industry has grown.

A Dangerous Obsession

Meet a dancer off-stage and the chances are they're 'off', suffering from stress-fractures, hairline fractures, brain fractures, or merely self-imposed anorexia. One might well wonder why any normal person would take up a career which has so many walking wounded.

Throughout history there have been accidents. A candle started a fire when Dauberval was dancing. Fellow dancer Dangui, three tailors and six stage-hands died, and Mlle Guimard, naked, grilled in her dressing room until a stagehand wrapped her in a curtain for her escape. Emma Livry, Taglioni's protégé, was not so lucky. Her dress caught fire from a gas-jet and she died a lingering death.

Quick thinking by dancers has saved situations; a ballerina whose nose was disjointed by a blow from her partner had it quickly knocked straight by fellow ballerina Freya Dominic. Michael Ho's knee was snapped back into place by a dancer on stage, and the audience didn't notice. Nor did they when Darcey Bussell braved her way with a damaged foot through the first night of the Royal Ballet production of *Sleeping Beauty* but couldn't make it through the *Grand pas de deux*. Maria Nunez slipped on and did it for her, and valiant Darcey took the curtain calls.

The audience did notice 17-year-old Fred Sharp's debut as an extra in *Romeo and Juliet* with the Joffrey Ballet. He fell ten feet through a trap-door and was then hit on the head by a candelabra in Juliet's funeral procession. He lived.

These are the major stage calamities. More damage is done in the daily class and rehearsals. Torn Achilles tendons are dramatic, but it is the groin and back strains which create gainful employment for a host of brilliant osteopaths and masseurs. Acquaint yourself with one of the best in case you sprain a wrist applauding.

BALLET MAKERS

You must acknowledge that certain choreographers are in a class of their own. Not only have they produced a huge number of great ballets, but these ballets have in turn influenced generations of other choreographers. There will be little argument as to who should fall into this category.

It is when discussing the second division that questions arise. Individual taste inevitably means that bluffers can simply insist that an 'also-ran' should be considered an 'all-time' because they have seen some obscure early work, or feel that their candidate has been unfairly neglected by press or managements. Such idle speculation can be most stimulating.

All-Time Greats (strictly alphabetical)

Ashton (1904-1988)

The irreplaceable Sir Fred, OM, CH, CBE, Ecuadorian born choreographer whose countless masterpieces are the essence of British ballet and whose curtain calls were an art form in themselves. He made versions of classic stories such as *Cinderella* created in 1948 for the beautiful red-headed and red shoe'd ballerina Moira Shearer and in which he and Sir Robert Helpmann were a monstrous pair of Ugly Sisters. Other hallmark works include:

Façade – Sir Fred at his elegant and wittiest best. Now over 70 years old it sparkles as much as William Walton's tunes, the Popular Song epitomising the weary camp world of the thirties.

Symphonic Variations – Pure geometry in motion, to César Franck's score, created in 1946. Go over the top with similes, celestial spheres and so on, specially if you saw the original cast.

Ondine – Originally saw the light of day in 1843 with choreography by Jules Perrot. Sir Fred created his version for Fonteyn to Hans Werner Henze's score in 1958. The only idea he retained was the *pas de l'ombre* in which Ondine sees her shadow for the first time. One of Fonteyn's greatest rôles, it's a classic story of a mortal torn between love for his earthly fiancée and a supernatural being (see *La Sylphide*) and has the usual tragic ending. In this case Ondine warns Palemon that if they kiss he'll die. They do. He does.

La Fille Mal Gardée – Always '*Fille*' to its friends, dates from 1789 when staged in France by Dauberval. 171 years later Ashton unveiled his version. Pure unadulterated pleasure. Sir Fred used every British theatre tradition to tell the very French story of Lise and her lover Colas and the problems they encounter before they can marry (principally Lise's mother, Widow Simone, whose choice of prospective son-in-law is rich farmer's son, Alain). There's a ribbon dance or two, a clog dance, a dance around the maypole, a dance with wine bottles and a live horse. The cock and hens are played by dancers, but in *Les Deux Pigeons*, Ashton's next ballet, he used two well-trained doves.

Fille's title defies catchy translation in spite of a competition once initiated by Madam to find one.

The Dream – One of Ashton's gems, but the practised will know it as the vehicle for launching the great Sibley/Dowell partnership in 1964. Set to Mendelssohn's music it is charmingly designed by the modern master of charming design, David Walker, who has worked similar wonders on Ashton's *Cinderella*, Mary Skeaping's *Giselle* and Peter Schaufuss's *La Sylphide*.

Out of a host of other works, you should rave about *Monotones I* and *II*, heavenly geometry again, *A Month in the Country*, which provided a great rôle for Lynn Seymour, and *Rhapsody*. Affect that you were at *Rhapsody's* first night on the occasion of the late Queen Mother's birthday, with Misha and Lesley (Collier) and showers of rose-petals.

Sir Fred was the master of the *pièce d'occasion* having previously mounted a beautiful solo to Elgar's *Salut d'Amour* for Dame Margot using steps from all the ballets he created for her (even the most assiduous ballet fan was severely challenged to identify them all).

Balanchine (1904-1983)

The 'all-American' choreographer from Georgia – Russia. The inimitable Mr. B. was creator of the all-American high-stepping ballerina. His association with Stravinsky was legendary; the Stravinsky Festival of 1972 was a high-point of American ballet. Wearing his cowboy boots, string tie and toggle, he looked as though he had stepped out of his own ballet, *Square Dance*. Latterly a specialist in plotless ballets which are pure movement, a few other key works include:

Apollo – Originally entitled *Apollon Musagète* it was created in 1928 and established neo-classicism. It showed the birth and youth of Apollo and his instruction of the muses of poetry, mime and dance. Dance wins hands down before he ascends Olympus to join the other gods. Celestial music by Stravinsky. Now in truncated form.

Serenade – The first ballet Mr. B. created when he went to the United States in 1934. It was made for students of the newly formed School of American Ballet and premièred in White Plains, New York State. You should know that the incidents which happened during its creation, a dancer falling, another arriving late, were kept in the finished version which closely follows the structure of the music, Tchaikovsky's *Serenade in C*.

Four Temperaments – Known as *Four T's*, is a melancholic, sanguine, phlegmatic, choleric ballet. Like many of Mr. B. ballets the original décor has long gone, and it is danced, to Hindemith's score, in practice clothes.

Bournonville (1805-1879)

Denmark's biggest export after Carlsberg and bacon, he trained in Denmark and Paris with his father, Antoine. He made his debut at the Paris Opéra in 1826, and returned to Denmark to become leading dancer for 20 years. His ballets convey moral messages in an appealing way, reflecting the motto which is over the stage at the Royal Theatre 'Ej blo til lyst' (Not only for amusement). He discovered the 16-year-old Lucille Grahn to be his Sylph, and quite possibly much more.

La Sylphide – Choreographed in 1836, it has outlived the original Paris production of 1832, never having been out of the repertoire of the Royal Danish Ballet for long. There is much discussion as to what has changed about it over the years, but you would be safe to pronounce, as Bournonville expert Erik Aschengreen does, "The only authentic performance is the first."

Bournonville could not afford to pay for the original music (by Schneitzhoeffer) so he commissioned the young Herman Lovensjold to write it anew (humming a few of the original tunes to inspire him), which he did triumphantly.

Far From Denmark – or Danes at Sea, is one of the Bournonville ballets which hasn't travelled – yet. Whether this tale of sailors from a Danish frigate anchored off Argentina will become as well loved as *La Sylphide* is a matter for conjecture. It contains a host of national dances, for eskimoes, chinese, indian temple dancers and red indians all of which, like his 'nigger dance' need to be performed with great period style to avoid being politically incorrect.

Kermesse in Bruges – High on the list of ballets which will sweep the world – one day. The title, The Fair At Bruges, is a non-starter. Three brothers set out to make their fortune, bearing with them three gifts from a merchant grateful to them for saving his daughter. One is given a magic ring which makes him irresistible to women; one (Adrian!) is given a sword which makes him invincible; while the third is given a lute which makes everyone dance – shades of *Salad Days*.

After many hilarious exploits the secret of the brothers' success gets out and the elder two and the merchant are arrested for sorcery. Just as they are about to be burned at the stake who should come along but the youngest and his magic lute. He makes everyone dance till they are exhausted (Look at me, Oh, look at me, Oh, look at me, I'm dancing...) and beg him to stop playing. He agrees, his brothers can go free and all ends, as they say, with general rejoicing. Completely idiotic stories like this make ballet worthy of serious study.

Napoli – Fishy, folksy goings-on in Naples. Boats come and go. On one, Gennaro, a fisherman, takes his bride for a ride, but is shipwrecked. She ends up in the Blue Grotto and is transformed, in the second act, into a naiad (see Glossary) by the King of the Sea. This act is referred to as the "Bronnum's act" because audiences found it so tedious they repaired for coffee to the café of that name next door to the Royal Theatre in Copenhagen, returning for the third act in which Gennaro, with a little help from the Madonna, saves her and all is rejoicing. The third act contains the only *pas de six* to be danced by ten.

Fokine (1880-1942)

Mikhail, dancer then choreographer with the Imperial Ballet, trained at the Maryinsky, and became the key choreographer with Diaghilev. He then produced his ballets for the various singular Ballet Russe companies which tried to keep the Diaghilev tradition alive.

Les Sylphides – Not to be confused with '*La*'. Positively soporific in some versions, this is the one about the poet, large floppy bow at throat, and his reverie in the woods. It is danced to Chopin tunes and was original entitled *Chopiniana* – indeed, still is, in Russia.

Le Spectre de la Rose – A young girl is asleep in her room after her first ball. She clutches a rose and dreams that its spirit dances with her, before taking a soaring leap out into the night. Created in 1911 for Nijinsky and Tamara Karsavina it takes equally great artists to avoid it drifting into embarrassing silliness.

Petrouchka – Spell it how you like, was created in 1911 for Nijinsky. Tamara was the Ballerina and Alexander Orlov was the Moor. It provides a great central rôle always cast from company stars, when in fact it can be more effectively danced by a good character dancer. The Magician manipulates his puppets for the benefit of the audience, but when the curtain comes down the dramas of the triangular relationship of Petrouchka,

Ballerina and Moor continue with tragic consequences. Just like life in the average ballet company.

Ivanov (1834-1901)

Worthy of inclusion in the pantheon of the greats on the strength of one and a half ballets. He joined the Imperial Ballet in St. Petersburg in 1852, and spent much of his career under the shadow of Petipa who took credit for much of his work. Ivanov created the most potent and powerful image in the world of ballet; the Swan Queen. For his efforts he got little reward in his lifetime and he died penniless and forgotten.

Nutcracker – Petipa's illness during the creation of this ballet in 1892 meant that Ivanov had complete creative control of the Snow Scene and the radiant *pas de deux*, which is all that is left of his original choreography. Today there are hundreds of different productions attacking E. T. A. Hoffmann's story and Tchaikovsky's music in as many ways. Outstanding recent productions have had innovative designs, in America by children's illustrator Maurice Sendak and in Britain by political cartoonist Gerald Scarfe.

Swan Lake – Petipa did the grand court scenes, but it is to Ivanov we must be grateful for the seminal images of the Swan Queen and her swan maidens in the second and fourth lakeside acts. The popular image of ballet.

Petipa (1818-1910)

The absolute monarch of the Tsar's Imperial Ballet for almost 35 years, he was born in Marseilles. He had a considerable career as a dancer in his father's company in Brussels and at the Comédie Française dancing with Carlotta Grisi (see Terrine de Ballet). He produced over 60 ballets and created the classic style which is the basis of ballet today.

Don Quixote – A full-length ballet which has little to do with the Don and a lot to do with Basilio, a barber and his love, Kitri. It was created in Moscow in 1869 to thumping tunes by Minkus, the Lloyd-Webber of 19th century ballet music. The *pas de deux* from the last act wedding celebrations is a gala favourite, giving otherwise tasteful dancers a chance to show off.

La Bayadère – Choreographed in 1877 to some made-to-measure tunes by Minkus. Only the Kingdom of the Shades scene is seen with any regularity outside Russia today. The famous entry of the temple dancers performing *arabesque penchée* followed by a back bend, filling the stage, is one of the most spectacular images in ballet. You scarcely need know that it is a tale of jealousy and lust in a Rajah's court which culminates with Nikiya, the temple dancer, being presented with a basket containing a poisonous snake to dispose of her which leaves Solor, her lover, free to marry the Rajah's daughter. As *Cléopatre* is no longer in the repertoire, this must now be considered the biggest asp disaster in the ballet world.

The Sleeping Beauty – Created in 1890, Tchaikovsky's music was not appreciated, and all the Tsar could bring himself to say was "Very nice". Now one of the three jewels of the classical crown, you will always refer to it as 'Beauty'.

Swan Lake – Only half Petipa, the court scenes and the national dances. What more is there to say about the ultimate ballet, except that bluffers should always refer to it as 'Lac'. This bit of its French title has stuck.

The most popular recent production was by Matthew Bourne, featuring Adam Cooper as Swan Queen and a flock of male swans.

Raymonda – Petipa's last great ballet, made in 1898, five years before his retirement, to ravishing music by the famous chemist, Glazunov. The story is so incredibly complicated that it is rarely performed complete outside Russia. The last act, the wedding celebrations of Raymonda and her Crusader lover, Jean de Brienne, is a glorious cascade of classical and Hungarian dance.

Raymonda loves Jean who is always crusading. He sends her, in lieu of a postcard, a tapestry of himself. In the meantime Abderame, a Saracen, tries to seduce her. After momentary temptation she spurns him and is rewarded by the appearance of a ghostly White Lady who conjures up a vision of Jean. But Abderame will not take no for an answer and tries to abduct her. Fortunately Jean and the King of Hungary, no less, arrive in the nick of time to rescue her. The King orders Jean and Abderame to fight for Raymonda, but when it looks as though the Saracen will win, the White Lady intervenes again to ensure that true love wins in the end.

Modern Masters

Béjart (b. 1922)

To the masses, a master of stagecraft and significance; to others a choreographer of hidden shallows. Arlene Croce of the *New Yorker* expressed serious opinion perfectly: 'pronounce his name Beige Art'.

Born in Marseilles, his early choreography was regarded as avant-garde in the fifties. His company became the Ballet of the Twentieth Century in 1960 at the Monnaie Theatre, Brussels, moved to Lausanne in

1985 and in 1992 transmogrified into the smaller Rudra Béjart. *The Ring Cycle,* is a five-hour ballet. It works, so declare it "A must!"

Ninth Symphony – Beethoven's, used to create a hymn for mankind. Multi-racial sentiments using oriental, asian and black dancers.

Boléro – Uses the music written for Ida Rubenstein by Ravel. Originally created for a single girl dancing on a huge round table surrounded by men, it has since been performed by a man surrounded by women and latterly, by a man surrounded by men. O tempora, O mores.

Cranko (1927-1973)

Born in the Transvaal, Cranko was a dancer, and very soon a choreographer, with the Sadlers Wells Ballet. Known for his inventive humour in the theatre with his revue *Cranks* in the fifties, as well as in his ballets. Became Director of the Stuttgart Ballet in 1961 (see Companies). Died on a plane flying from New York to Stuttgart.

Pineapple Poll – Adapted from W. S. Gilbert's Bab Ballad, The Bumboat Woman's Story, the music is Sullivan arranged by Charles Mackerras and the scenery by Osbert Lancaster in his inimitable style which would later decorate *Fille*. Poll is infatuated by the devastatingly handsome Captain Belaye and is in turn loved by the pot boy, Jasper. Poll and her friends disguise themselves as sailors and board Belaye's ship. But he returns with his bride and her chattering Aunt Dimple. Much confusion ensues, but eventually all is becalmed. Belaye promotes himself to Admiral and as a consolation prize Jasper becomes a Captain. As a result Poll agrees to marry him. She is clearly a social climber.

Onegin – An unsung masterpiece created for the Stuttgart Ballet in 1965. The rôle of Tatyana was passionately danced by Natasha Makarova for several of her positively last farewell performances. Also by Josephine Jewkes at English National Ballet (ENB). Music by Tchaikovsky, but not from the opera of the same name. Ballet bluffers should note that *Onegin* is pronounced 'on-yay-gin' with a hard 'g' and should not sound like an interval drink.

MacMillan (1929-1992)

Sir Kenneth, former Director of the Royal Ballet. Born in Dunfermline, he forged his father's signature on the application for his first audition. Trained at Royal Ballet School and danced with Sadler's Wells. Prolific producer of ballets, many inspired by Lynn Seymour and, later, mega-dramatic Russian Irek Mukhamedov, OBE, who made his Royal debut in a solo from *Winter Dreams,* based on Chekov's *Three Sisters,* and *The Judas Tree* one of the few ballets set on a building site. His last work was the dances for the acclaimed musical revival of *Carousel* at National Theatre, London, and on Broadway.

The Invitation – Set some time before the First World War, a young girl and her cousin are seduced during a house-party by an unhappy married couple. Started the great partnership of Seymour and Christopher Gable in 1960.

Anastasia – Began life as a one-act ballet in Berlin in 1967, to music by Martinu. Everyone thought Lynn Seymour sensational in the title rôle and some thought a three-act ballet was crying to get out. MacMillan obviously agreed because he produced exactly that for the Royal Ballet in 1971. He used Tchaikovsky's Symphonies 1 and 3 for the additional two acts which show the Grand Duchess Anastasia's life at court before she is discovered in a mental home in act three. Everyone thought Seymour sensational. Some thought a one-act ballet was crying to get back in.

Manon – A modern masterpiece created for the Royal Ballet in 1974, the music is by Massenet, but not from *Manon* the opera. It is a glorious pot pourri of works ranging from *Cendrillon* to the sensuous *Valse très lente*, beautifully melded together by Leighton Lucas. Manon is the original good-time girl who, swamped with riches at the beginning, eventually lands up in a swamp at the end.

In love with Des Grieux, a poet, she accepts money to live with a rich gentleman, but not before a night of passion and a *pas de deux* in the poet's bedroom. Manon plans to run away with him, but the gentleman arranges to have them arrested. Manon is sent to a penal colony, the faithful poet following her just in time to rescue her from the amorous intentions of her jailer. Escaping through swamps Manon catches fever, but summons up enough energy to dance a final *pas de deux*.

Elite Syncopations – A romp created in 1974 at the height of the Scott Joplin craze. Widely performed, it was a case of rags to riches for MacMillan.

Massine (1895-1979)

You could say that Leonide Massine should be classed as an all-time great. That he isn't, may simply be whim of fashion. Born in Moscow, he trained at the Imperial School, joined the Diaghilev enterprise to dance in *The Legend of Joseph* in 1913, and didn't look back. No wonder: he was Diaghilev's principal choreographer and greatest passion. After Diaghilev's death he was associated with the various Ballet Russe companies, becoming noted for his 'symphonic' ballets. Pronounce him the Russian way – 'Mee-ass-in'.

Parade – Cocteau concocted a scenario, in response to Diaghilev's request "Astonish me!", involving performers trying to attract an audience. The cubist decor was by Picasso and the score, by Erik Satie, included passages for a typewriter.

La Boutique Fantasque – Created in 1919 to Rossini tunes it concerns a toy shop in which dolls come to life to help a pair of can-can dancers who have been sold to different families. Apart from an insufferable poodle (you should pity the dancer cast in this leg-raising part) the ballet is best described as a romp.

Nijinska (1891-1972)

Sister of Nijinsky and Diaghilev's choreographer in the early twenties, she created two key works.

Les Noces – Made in 1923 to a Stravinsky score, as a series of tableaux showing a Russian peasant wedding, designed in sombre browns by Natalia Goncharova, it is an equally sombre and deeply devotional piece. Sir Frederick Ashton brought Nijinska to the Royal Ballet to re-create it some 40 years after its first performance.

Les Biches – The epitome of twenties chic (as was her *Train Bleu*) heightened by Poulenc's bright score. It is a little bit naughty with hints of lesbianism. Assume that just about everybody remembers how brilliant Svetlana Beriosova was, brandishing a long cigarette holder and swinging her long string of pearls, in the role of the Hostess.

De Mille (1909-1993)

Agnes, niece of Cecil B. the movie mogul, trained partly with Rambert in London. Her ballets include *Fall River Legend* (Lizzie Borden took an axe...) and *Rodeo* which together with others such as Loring's *Billy the Kid*, are the first American national ballets. They led directly to the first serious ballet in a musical – *Laurie makes up her mind* in *Oklahoma*.

Nijinsky (1888-1950)

An all-time great dancer and innovative choreographer, though only one of his ballets is performed today.

L'Après-midi d'un Faune – Made in 1912 it is still danced, long outliving the scandal caused by the use to which the faun put the scarf dropped by a nymph, thus bringing the ballet to a climax. It is also notable for Nijinsky's odd choreographic ideas which involved the dancers walking in profile as though they had stepped down from an Egyptian frieze.

Le Sacre du Printemps – First saw the light of day at the Théatre de Champs Elysées in 1913. Stravinsky's music caused such an uproar that it could hardly be heard by the dancers; Nijinsky had to shout out the complicated rhythms from the wings. As the dancers performed the contorted rhythmic steps a member of the audience shouted "Un dentiste", another added "Deux dentistes" after which it was downhill all the way according to Dame Marie Rambert who was there. It is now regarded as a breakthrough in choreography.

Robbins (1918-1998)

The Mr. Broadway of the ballet. From his first work *Fancy Free* (which became the musical *On the Town*) 'Jerry' has moved easily between the ballet and musical stages. He became Mr. B.'s Associate Director at City Ballet in 1949 and produced a stream of ballets including *The Cage*, *Afternoon of a Faun* and *The Concert*. He choreographed the *Little House of Uncle Tom* ballet in *The King and I* and with *West Side Story* in 1957, changed the course of the musical. His sheer facility has brought praise and some criticism. Usually from those without it.

Afternoon of a Faun – Uses the same Debussy score as Nijinsky's version. The faun is a narcissistic male dancer asleep on the floor of a ballet studio, the nymphs replaced by a ballerina. The gimmick is that the audience is watching the ballet through the rehearsal mirror and that the two dancers only look at each other in the same mirror. The ballerina leaves, the faun awakes. Was it all a dream?

Dances at a Gathering – A plotless ballet to Chopin piano pieces which is a hallmark Robbins' work. Robbins insists it has no plot, but from the moment when the first man puts his hand tenderly on the ground it is clearly a ballet about settlers in a new land. The American experience?

Tudor (1909-1987)

Virtual inventor of the 'psychological' ballet, Antony Tudor started out as general handyman and dancer with the fledgling Rambert company in the 1930s, where he created *Gala Performance* and *Lilac Garden*.

Worked in America during and after the Second World War with Ballet Theatre creating *Pillar of Fire* and *Undertow*. Long fallow periods, but made a triumphant comeback in 1967 with *Shadowplay* for the Royal Ballet. With his sparse and economical style reflected in his private life, it was no surprise that he died in a Buddhist retreat.

Lilac Garden – An archetypal Tudor ballet. Created in 1936, this taut drama set to Chausson's *Poème* was a trail-blazing psychological ballet of relationships. The frozen moment in time when the complex emotions of Caroline, her Lover, the Man She Must Marry and the Women in His Past sums up the powerful ballet. Caroline never gets close enough to say goodbye to her Lover until the party is almost over and he puts a sprig of lilac into her hand. But Caroline must marry, so she has to leave him. They'll never gather lilac in the wings again.

Bluffers will want to add their own candidates to this list, and there are some with the sort of influence to merit it. You could propose the double Dutch duo **van Manen** and **van Dantzig**; **Kylian**; **Lavrovsky**, creator of the Bolshoi *Romeo and Juliet*; **Grigorovich** of *Spartacus* fame, or the ubiquitous **Ronald Hynd** whose ballets are danced across three continents.

Then there is the new generation starting with **David Bintley**, great hope of British choreography and creator of much-praised works such as *The Snow Queen* and *Hobson's Choice*.

Current favourite is **William (Billy) Forsythe** who *Somewhat Elevated* companies world wide, including his own in Frankfurt.

Names to Drop

Lists of ballet personalities and biographies of dancers are easily come by, but it is always handy to have a few truly obscure alongside the genuinely interesting.

Carina Ari – Swedish ballerina of the short-lived Ballet Suedois, who died in 1970 leaving her fortune (she married into the Bols liqueur family) to a foundation named after her. It cossetts already overcossetted Swedish dancers. A lot of Bols.

Lord Berners – Eccentric British composer of Ashton's *A Wedding Bouquet*. Kept a piano in the back of his Rolls Royce and a flock of rainbow-dyed doves. Full name Gerald Tyrwhitt-Wilson which says it all.

Arlette van Boven – Belgian dancer, former Director of NDT2 (see Ballet Companies). Brilliant administrator, teacher, talent spotter and ballet news gatherer. Pure Leo.

Les Deux Christophe – Ex-Royal **Christopher Wheeldon** left for Boston and New York City Ballet to make his name as a choreographer. The Royal brought him back for a *Tryst* – a perfect match. **Christopher Hampson** (Hampy to bluffers) stayed with ENB and created *Double Concerto*, the *Etudes* of today, followed by ENB's new *Nutcracker*. Other projects include *Romeo and Juliet* for the Royal New Zealand Ballet.

Adam Glushkovsky – Truly a name to bandy about. Dancer and teacher in Moscow and St. Petersburg at the beginning of the 1800s. Best known for saving the Moscow Ballet School two days before Napoleon's troops reached the city in 1812.

Beryl Grey – Tall, striking Royal Ballet ballerina who danced her first full-length *Swan Lake* on her 15th birthday in 1943. As Director of London Festival Ballet from 1968 to 1980 was noted for her double entendres, mostly unprintable.

Anders Hellstrom – Swedish 'dark horse'. Dancer with Neumeier and Forsythe, director of Gothenburg Ballet. Predict that he will turn up somewhere important.

Robert Joffrey – For years kept his small company together in New York bringing many Ashton ballets to America. One of very few choreographers of Afghan descent, born Abdullah Jaff Anver Bey Khan.

Jules Léotard – French acrobat who invented the the well-known rehearsal garment.

Serge Lifar – Glamour boy of the Diaghilev Ballet after Dolin. Architect of French ballet post-Diaghilev, though few of his ballets are performed now apart from *Suite en Blanc*. Founded his own University of the Dance and was prone to give out hand-written diplomas at parties.

Joseph Maillot – Costumier at the Paris Opéra in the early 1800s. Inventor of tights which became widely used. In theatres in the Pope's domain they had to be blue, not flesh-coloured.

Alicia Markova – Diaghilev's 'little English girl' trained by Astafieva in her famous King's Road studio where fellow student Patrick Healey-Kay pinched her and pulled her hair. Founded London Festival Ballet with Healey-Kay, by then called Dolin. Directed the Metropolitan Opera Ballet. Was filmed still tirelessly lecturing, teaching and coaching when well into in her 90s. A fund of anecdotes, many collected in *Markova Remembers* – a bluffing necessity.

Charles Mudry – Ballet master extraordinaire. Swiss born, Russian-trained teacher of a generation of fine young dancers, mostly Swedish. After fiveyears with Neumeier in Hamburg, now guest teacher with NDT, ENB, Royal Danish, New Zealand and Swedish. Can say 'cheese' in 13 languages.

Anna Pavlova – Took ballet to places no pointe shoe had trod before. In Hollywood she was filmed with Douglas Fairbanks; Frederick Ashton saw her in Peru; in New Zealand her name was given to a sumptuous meringue confection.

Paul Taylor – Wonderfully witty modern dance choreographer whose *Aureole* is in the repertoire of many classical companies to give the impression of being progressive.

Stanley Williams – The svengali of male dance teaching and guru to the greats. English born, but brought up in Denmark (where he became expert in the Bournonville style), his devotees never travelled far without a cassette of his class in their baggage.

Wayne Sleep – Vertically challenged, outstanding product of the Royal Ballet, Britain's greatest populariser of the dance. Perfect example of Béjart's 'bad fairy' theory: to be blessed with brilliant technique, but insufficient inches to do the premier danseur rôles. After a spectacular ballet career began an equally spectacular career in musical theatre from *Cats* to pantomimes. If you saw Princess Diana dancing with Wayne at the Royal Opera House, mention it as often as possible.

BALLET COMPANIES

Ballet companies have personalities just as much as dancers, sometimes reflecting their history, sometimes that of their founder. Bluffers should have a little knowledge of the background and flavour of major companies to avoid any obvious mistakes. For example, no ballet lover would admit to having admired Maurice Béjart's various companies without a well-practised sneer at the same time; no aficionado would think that a reference to 'City Ballet' referred to any other city than New York, no matter how much they think of Vienna City Ballet.

Companies have their ups and downs and the wheel of fortune can have the Royal Ballet riding high in critical acclaim one season and being criticised unmercifully the next, for little apparent reason other than that the focus of interest has moved elsewhere. But all companies live with the knowledge that the wheel keeps on turning.

They are awarded Bluffer's Guide points (1-5).

The Bolshoi

Bolshoi means big and that's the way they dance, though the name actually refers to the theatre. Now in a state of disrepair as funds from the state racecourse monopoly have gone private. Should you wish to eulogise their bravura style, always manage to hint that you really prefer the pure classicism of the Kirov.

Though ballet at the Bolshoi dates from the 1770s, today's company is very much the product of the Russian Revolution. The first Commissioner for Enlightenment allowed the company to continue, even though it epitomised the reign of the Tsars. The first Soviet ballet was *The Red Poppy*, the story of a

Chinese dancer who saves the life of a Soviet ship's captain who brought grain to her land during a coolie uprising. Pure poetry. Other epics followed, not least Grigorovich's *Spartacus*.

Their first appearance in the West in 1956 was a milestone of ballet history; *Romeo and Juliet* with Ulanova and Fadeyechev. If you wish to bluff that you saw it, get the video or see the film.

Current performances can be bolshoi rag-bags with so many dancers appearing at so many venues at the same time. Rating: BG 4 for being so Bolshoi.

The Kirov

The company always felt one-up on the Bolshoi, being the true Imperial Ballet when it was known as the Maryinsky (take care to refer to Maryinsky style, rather than Kirov style when, for instance, discussing the works of Balanchine or the heritage of the Royal Ballet). The home of the classical style which is the basis of all the 20th-century companies in the West, Mikhail Fokine created half-a-dozen seminal works at the Maryinsky before he opted for the West after the 1917 Revolution. The eminent teacher Vaganova kept his spirit alive and in 1957 the Kirov School was named after her. There are too many star graduates to list here, but any programme note will inform bluffers of who they are.

July 1961 brought the Kirov to the West; an unforgettable occasion when 32 perfectly-schooled Kirov ballerinas slowly came on stage doing *penchée arabesque* after *penchée arabesque* until it was filled for the opening of the Kingdom of the Shades act of *La Bayadère*.

The Kirov, unlike the Bolshoi, suffered serious defections of which bluffers will be only too aware, for they helped change the face of ballet in the West. Nureyev, Natasha (Makarova) and Misha left for artistic freedom and a greater range of designer clothes. After a minor identity crisis it is reasserting itself and forging links with Western dancers and companies. Now that Leningrad is St. Petersburg once again, speculate that it may not be long before the Kirov becomes the Maryinsky.

BG 5, in spite of occasional artistic lapses.

American Ballet Theatre (sic)

When Misha and Natasha defected, it was to ABT, as the company is always known, that they fled. To audiences across America this is known as the 'national' company since it has always toured extensively, bringing many foreign dancers to its audience; Alicia and Pat (Markova and Dolin) during World War II and after, Erik and Carla (Bruhn and Fracci) and others. They gave an early stage to Antony Tudor as well as, later, Twyla Tharp and MacMillan (Sir Kenneth) with his, then muse, Alex (Alessandra Ferri), now big in Milan.

ABT have a basic repertoire of the classics, including Misha's *Cinderella*, allegedly the most expensive ballet production ever. Now and then management disputes have overshadowed performances by such greats as Fernando (Bujones), Cynthia (Gregory) and Gelsey (Kirkland), who came and went like yoyos.

In the late 1990s the company played safe under the financial direction of Michael Kaiser (who came and went like a yoyo at the Royal Opera House where in 2001 he installed his protégée, Australian Ross Stretton). A name to drop is that of charming star, Ethan Steifel, who not only guests at the Royal, but was the perfect Colas in ABT's *La Fille Mal Gardée*, rehearsed by Alexander Grant, the original Alain, who inherited the ballets *Fille* and *Façade* from Sir Fred.

BG rating: only 3 points for varying fortunes.

New York City Ballet

'City Ballet' was very much the personal empire of George Balanchine and the seriously rich Lincoln Kirstein, who invited him to America in 1935. They first formed the School of American Ballet, which still supplies the company with long-legged thoroughbreds (ballerinas, that is). One-time Balanchine ballerina Gelsey Kirkland has documented in painful detail the agonies some dancers go through to achieve the Mr. B. look: uppers and downers and methods not entirely fit for polite society to discuss.

City Ballet was founded in 1948 and is now based at Lincoln Center. After Mr. B.'s death in 1985 it was directed by one of his oldest collaborators Jerome (Jerry to bluffers) Robbins and then one of his star dancers, Peter Martins, who has given many other young choreographers their chances.

BG rating: 5 points is a must.

The Royal Ballet

It is something of a conceit that this company assumes everyone knows where it comes from. It was not even the first company to be given a Royal Charter; the Royal Winnipeg had theirs three years earlier.

It was founded by Dame Ninette de Valois (Edris Stannus, as was) who you always refer to as 'Madam', as does everyone else After her years with Diaghilev she produced dances at the Old Vic Theatre before starting her school at Sadler's Wells Theatre. To know of its subsequent growth provides good bluffing

45

material. In the beginning was the Vic-Wells (1931), which begat the Sadler's Wells (1940), which begat the Sadler's Wells Theatre Ballet (1945) which, on receipt of a Royal Charter in 1956, begat The Royal Ballet. This in turn begat several offspring on the Sadler's Wells theme, such as the Touring company that nurtured great talents including Christopher Gable, and ended up as the Birmingham Royal Ballet (BRB). The Royal itself stayed put at Covent Garden.

Madam directed the company until 1963, to be followed by Sir Fred, who bluffers can hint was not of directorial bent, then Kenneth MacMillan, Norman Morrice (ex-Rambert) and Anthony Dowell. After a short tenure, Australian Ross Stretton exited dramatically and was succeeded by Monica Mason, the original doomed Chosen Maiden in MacMillan's *Rite of Spring,* who was faced with the task of sorting a muddled repertoire and placating the not very happy dancers. Bluffers are aware that she has been a success at both.

The company is the guardian of the priceless Ashton repertoire (though you might hint that this guardianship is a bit wanting) and has the major MacMillan works carefully protected by Lady Deborah MacMillan. You are allowed to disparage the attempts to breathe new life into classics by Anthony Dowell. More the kiss of death.

Dredging up the past provides pure gold for seasoned bluffers. If you saw the roster of great ballerinas, Beryl Grey, Nadia Nerina, Svetlana Beriosova, Merle Park, Lynn Seymour and Antoinette Sibley, you can name-drop to your heart's content. A rare sighting, which wins hands down, is that of Moira Shearer in *Cinderella,* casting that true bluffers will know sent the Prima Ballerina Assoluta, Margot Fonteyn, to France with Roland Petit and, more importantly, Christian Dior (the equivalent nowadays of Darcey Bussell and Sylvie Guillem promoting a rather heavy watch which must surely affect their *ports de bras*.) Home-grown favourites such as Viviane Durante and Sarah Wilder have departed through neglect.

Always have a Bobbie Helpmann anecdote to hand. He was the first of a formidable male team; Michael Somes, David Blair, Alexander Grant, David Wall, Christopher Gable and Anthony Dowell. These days there are few names to drop, though there are brilliant dancers, like Adam Cooper who made it by leaving to become Odette in Matthew Bourne's all male *Swan Lake*. Instead, bone up on guest artistes Roberto Bolle from La Scala (who took part in the Party at the Palace for the Queen's Jubilee in 2002), Carlos Acosta and Ethan Steifel from ABT, and the incomparable Dane, Johan Kobborg. Serious bluffers will know of his low key debut in Scottish Ballet's *La Sylphide* before quietly storming the British ballet scene. Bluffer's are encouraged to wonder out loud when Madam's beloved Royal Ballet School will produce a crop of male principal dancers to match the current roster of stars from far shores.

Patchy is the best description, so BG rating: 4.

Nederlands Dans Theater

One of the greatest of modern dance companies, included in these pages because it was, and is, so firmly classically based. Founded in 1959 by a group from the Dutch National Ballet including Ben Harkarvy and Hans van Manen. Recently directed by Czech choreographer and mushroom fancier Jiri Kylian, it is now in a transition period, providing opportunities for names to drop. Producing more new works a season than any other company, its younger version (NDT2), when under the direction of Arlette van Boven, produced a new generation of choreographers, Natcho Duarto, Ohad Naharin, Paul Lightfoot, all names worth mentioning. Ms. van Boven went on to direct NDT3 for oldies (dancers, that is).

BG rating: definitely 5 for being in a class of its own.

Royal Danish Ballet

One hundred and fifty years are summed up by the name 'Bournonville'. From that time the man and his influence have been the essence of Danish ballet. He not only created ballets which are still around today, but also the style in which they are performed. He also created a multi-currency industry ahead of his time. Sadly for him, royalties are not payable.

Auguste Bournonville took over as director, choreographer, dancer and social conscience in 1829, giving up dancing in 1848, but keeping the other posts as absolute monarch until 1875, which means he is only two generations away – in ballet terms, quite close really.

His company continued the tradition of making male dancing respectable. Great dancers included Erik Bruhn, Henning Kronstam, Niels Kehlet, Flemming Flindt and Peter Schaufuss, all useful names if you saw them perform. Ballerinas did not lag far behind: Margot Lander, Toni Lander (they shared a husband), Mona Vangsaae (Ashton's Juliet and mother of Peter Schaufuss), Vivi Flindt and Anna Laerkesen, who was born to be the Sylph.

Directors that have come and gone include Niels Bjorn Larsen (always refer to him as ballet's greatest mime) and Harald Lander (creator of *Etudes*). Then there were Frank Schaufuss, Flindt, Kronstam and briefly Peter Schaufuss, stepping into his father's shoes. Frank Andersen inherited this poisoned chalice in 2002. Directors here have a hard task under the shadow of Bournonville and heavily unionised dancers.

BG rating: 3 for just being there so long.

English National Ballet

Founded as Festival Ballet by Alicia Markova and Anton Dolin with a brilliant impresario, Dr. Julian Braunsweg, whose scurrilous memoirs are a fund of information for bluffers. Best anecdotes come from Doris Barry, his assistant. You will know that she is Markova's sister, one of four. Later directors included Donald Albery (point out that Donmar Theatre, home of great productions was named after 'Don'-ald and 'Mar'-got Fonteyn, who jointly owned the warehouse, as it then was). He was followed by John Gilpin (Britain's answer to Erik Bruhn), Beryl Grey, John Field (ex-Royal) and then Peter Schaufuss, the most charismatic occupant of the post who changed the name to ENB and founded the school, for which he is given little credit. He was ousted by Pamela, Lady Harlech, who is not a name to drop for she brought in Ivan Nagy (pronounced Narge) who frittered away the inheritance. Derek Deane then did a brilliant job revitalising dancers and creating the 'arena' ballets at the Royal Albert Hall, until he left through ill-health and was replaced by the Swede, Matz Skoog.

Festival Ballet introduced many foreign dancers to Britain. But bluffers beware. Names such as Toumanova, Danilova, Goviloff and Flindt will date you. André Prokovsky and Galina Samsova led the company in the late 60s. Schaufuss starred in the early 70s with America's 'lost' ballerina, Dagmar Kessler. She arrived in Europe aged 18 and was soon snapped up to partner John Gilpin. She arrived, he left, and so, by chance, the magical Kessler/Schaufuss partnership was born, filling the Royal Festival Hall with audiences and showers of flowers. As a result

America was deprived of a great ballerina who only returned to make guest performances. Their reign lasted until the mid-70s. Schaufuss returned in 1978 to mount *La Sylphide,* commissioned by Beryl Grey and, later, Sir Fred's *Romeo and Juliet* in which he had danced the Page, at the age of seven.

Today the company is led by Estonian ballerina Agnes Oakes and ballet's best kept secret, her husband, Thomas Edur, one of the greatest classical dancers of modern times.

BG rating: 4, for being audience friendly and having dancers who work like hell.

Scottish Ballet

Deserving a mention for past successes, the company was the creation of Peter Darrell after the demise of his (and Liz West's) ground-breaking Western Theatre Ballet. Few of his creations remain in the repertoire other than his *Swan Lake*, where the 'white acts' are a drug induced fantasy. His one-time associate director was Elaine MacDonald, Britain's greatest home-grown dramatic ballerina.

Under 2002 director, ex-Royal Ashley Page, wondering whether to be classical or modern.

BG rating: 1 point until they sort themselves out.

Australian Ballet

Today's company is the successor of several small groups from the 1940s formed by dancers from various Ballet Russe companies who settled there.

The Australian Ballet's first performance was in November 1962 with a British inclined repertoire including Ashton and Cranko (note Madam's influence). In 1964, Robert Helpmann, her "odd little antipodean" created the first 'Australian' ballet, *The Display*, about the vain mating habits of the lyre bird. Perfect for Australian male dancers. A school was opened which produced great dancers such as Marylin Rowe and John Meehan. Helpmann took over the reins in 1974 and Anne Woolliams, influential head of the school, took over from him in 1976.

Maina Gielgud, niece of Sir John and former dancer with Béjart and Festival, succeeded her and enjoyed a particularly successful 10 years until she was ungraciously told that her contract would not be renewed. Thanks indeed. Under her leadership you will know that the company acquired world status with works by Kylian and Tetley as well as native pieces by Graeme Murphy of Sydney Dance Company, including his breathtaking *Nutcracker,* partly set in Melbourne. Pupils from the school regularly sweep up prizes at international ballet competitions. David McAllister took over as director in 2002.

Rating: BG 2, while marking time.

The Royal New Zealand Ballet

Founded 1961, but before this NZ dancers had made their mark abroad, notably Royal Ballet ballerina Rowena Jackson, who married Briton Philip Chatfield (who was tall enough to partner Beryl Grey). Alexander Grant, New Zealand's greatest export after kiwi fruit, was already an established soloist at the Royal Ballet, as his younger brother, Gary would also become. Recent directors such as Skoog (see ENB) had more luck keeping home talent, as well as tempting Grant back to produce Ashton's *Fille*. The company boasts one of ballet's few dancing knights, Sir Jon Trimmer. Gary Harris currently lords it as director.

BG rating: 3 for determination and for doing so much, so well, so far away, even from Australia.

National Ballet of Canada

Founded by Celia Franca on the suggestion of Madam (again) in 1951. Based in Toronto it has a large school which produces most of its dancers. Headed for some years by Karen Kain, Canada's national treasure, and her partner, Frank Augustyn. Attempts to develop a 'Canadian' repertoire have not been successful (bluffers should investigate Royal Winnipeg and Grands Ballets Canadiens for that) and they have relied on blockbusters by Petit, Nureyev's *Sleeping Beauty*, which almost bankrupted them, and Peter Schaufuss's *Napoli* (with help from Bournonville) bravely commissioned by Alexander Grant. A big gamble which paid off. As long ago as 1987 they dived down a rabbit hole with Tetley's *Alice*.

BG rating: only 2, until they dig themselves out of that hole.

Paris Opéra Ballet

From the 1930s-50s run by egomaniac Serge Lifar with Yvette Chauviré as prima ballerina. Nureyev's direction produced more press material than lasting ballets. The school, small by international standards, is a centre of excellence. A list of graduates would fill several pages. Best known is Sylvie Guillem famous for her 'six o'clock' legs. Now a Principal Guest with the Royal Ballet, watch out for her partner, Nicholas la Riche, a name to drop if ever there was one. If you saw their *Marguerite and Armand*, flaunt the fact.

A perfect BG 5 for technical skill, and style by the mile.

Ballet de Marseille

The creation of Roland Petit, it has all the show-biz flair associated with this most French of French choreographers, now in active retirement in Geneva.

After early Parisian successes such as his classic *Carmen*, made for his wife Zizi Jeanmaire, he was lured to Hollywood. In the 1950s he created a 17-minute ballet for Zizi in Danny Kaye's *Hans Christian Andersen* and memorable dances for Leslie Caron in *Daddy Long Legs*. Back on the ballet stage he made his enjoyable version of the Saint-Leon/Delibes' *Coppélia*. Enthuse about the score. In it the eccentric old inventor became a white-tied Astaire. The dance with his living doll, Coppélia, is comedy and pathos entwined. Pure Fred and Ginger. Sadly many of Petit's ballets don't travel well. For some it is dancing chic, too chic.

Give them BG 2 points while they recover from the founder's departure.

Ballet Rambert/Rambert Dance Company

The child of the formidable Marie Rambert, almost a match of Ninette de Valois. She was a Polish dancer with Diaghilev and admitted to being in love with Nijinsky when she helped him mount *Rite of Spring*. She opened a studio in London in 1920, that led to the Ballet Rambert and the Ballet Club, that gave performances at the tiny, but famous, Mercury Theatre, in now-fashionable Notting Hill in London. Bluffers will recognise it (and a brief glimpse of Mim, as she was known) in *The Red Shoes*. 'To Dance is to Live'. Get the T-shirt.

It was Mim who discovered all the creators who helped Madam make, eventually, the Royal Ballet. She fought to keep her company going until 1966, but the huge cost of mounting classics finished her. You will know that it was Ballet Rambert that introduced Bournonville's *La Sylphide* to Britain. The company then went modern on the Nederlands' model.

Head and shoulders above directors has stood Christopher Bruce. Former dancer with the company, he created a personal vision ranging from *Ghost Dances* (which brought the haunting South American pan pipes to public attention) to his wildly popular *Rooster* using Rolling Stones songs.

Deserves a BG 4 for innovation and getting bums on seats for dance.

Royal Swedish Ballet

Rarely adventuring abroad (they are so well looked after that they can't bear the inconvenience), this is a fine company with fine dancers and the best 'pick 'n mix' repertoire in Europe. But they keep it to themselves. Seek it out. It ranges from Robbins' *Les Noces* to Beryl Grey's *Sleeping Beauty*. They boasted two of the greatest dancers in Anneli Alhanko (Finnish actually) and Per-Arthur Segerstrom.

To make it in the international scene, dancers have had to leave. A short list will give bluffers good material: Johann Renvall (ABT), Tim Almaas (ENB), Petter Jacobsson (BRB), Matz Skoog (ENB, dancer and director) and Anders Hellstrom (Gothenburg).

In the hope that they can get their act together with new director Madeleine Onne, BG 3.

Stuttgart Ballet

Deserving a listing for past glories, it was created by John Cranko for his muse, Marcia Haydée and her American partner, Richard Cragun. His legacy is worth bluffing about, if only because it is not performed so much apart from *Onegin*. It is difficult for them to recreate the heady days of its founder, who died on a plane in 1973. Stuttgart was then known as 'Cranko's Castle'. Older bluffers are allowed to carry on about *Cranks*, Mr. Cranko's break from ballet into revue.

BG rating: 2 points, but bluffers must always hope for more because they are sure to find direction.

The Berlin Ballet

The arrival of Peter Schaufuss in Berlin galvanised a sleeping giant, but not for long. Links were formed with the Kirov and his new production of *Giselle* was greeted with acclaim. Based at the Deutsche Oper, they were not to know that the Staats Oper (in the former East) was being predatory. Bluffers will know that there is no room for two mega companies in a city this size. Schaufuss moved on (see below).

Perhaps the last great event was Nureyev's final performance – not dancing, but conducting Béjart's *Song of a Wayfarer*, danced by Schaufuss and Patrick Dupond, then director of the Paris Opéra Ballet.

BG rating: 1 point, until the East/West business is sorted out.

Peter Schaufuss Balletten

Having danced world-wide, directed ENB, Berlin and Royal Danish, Schaufuss now has his own company in the tiny Danish city of Holstebro. Ponder about how many cities of comparable size could support an orchestra, drama company and major ballet company. He also started a school, among whose talented pupils is his son, Luke, the third of this dancing dynasty, already stagewise.

He produces three-acters almost twice a year. They range from the *Tchaikovsky Trilogy* to *Midnight Express* (one of the few S&M ballets) plus *Elvis, the King; She Loves You* (Beatles) and, in 2003, *Diana, The Princess*.

BG rating: 5 for serious achievement while fitting in a lot of golf at the same time.

Hamburg Ballet

John Neumeier sounds German, but bluffers will know he hails from Milwaukee. Hugely prolific his is a total dedication to dance, creating, collecting (you should know of his huge collection of Nijinsky memorablia) and performing. After being a dancer in Stuttgart, he did his 'own thing', firstly in Frankfurt, where he created *Romeo and Juliet* and *Nutcracker*. In 1973 he moved to Hamburg where he still is, complete with specially built theatre, a thriving school and dedicated staff and dancers. His ballet master, the *wunderkind*, Kevin Haigen, starred in Neumeier's recreation of *Legend of Joseph* (Strauss) for the Vienna Staats Oper and is a noted teacher.

A perfect BG 5 points for talent and tenacity.

Nureyev and Friends

Not strictly a company, but an excuse for ballet lovers to remember Rudolf Nureyev (1938-1993), the dancer of the age. He toured with friends, but will always be remembered for magnificent performances with companies (particularly the RB) and the magic of the dance with Fonteyn. He improved male dance and made a whole generation of male dancers pull their jocks up. You may recall the chanting at the Royal Opera House, "We want Rudi. Preferably in the nudie."

Russian Roulette

At one time you would have referred to Russian dancers as a generality. Now any seasoned bluffer will be precise, especially if in conversation with the dancer involved. There are Estonian dancers (the most notable being ENB's Thomas Edur and Agnes Oakes), Latvians including Misha, Lithuanian father and daughter 'Papa' and Svetlana Beriosova, and the Kirov's divine Kazakhistani, Altynai Asylmuratova.

And there are, of course, still 'Russian' dancers, those being born in the Russian Republic centring on St. Petersburg and Moscow. The far-flung parts of the old Russian Empire have always produced great dancers, from Nureyev who was born on a train near Irtursk, to the young Pavlova who won the 1973 Moscow Competition, who came from Perm in the Urals. Remember that these national centres have schools of excellence, though the best talent is inevitably drawn to St. Petersburg or the Bolshoi in Moscow. "He/she trained at Vaganova" is a good ploy as many balletomanes can't remember in which city this great school is based (St. Petersburg).

Après La Danse

At one time crowds waited outside the stage door to meet their favourites and they would not be disappointed. With perfect make-up (not only the ballerinas) and dressed impeccably, from Markova to Makarova (silk chiffon scarf a-flowing), they would graciously sign autographs and accept flowers.

Sadly stage-door glamour has waned. Nowadays the crowds are smaller, affording a better chance of meeting dancers, but only consummate bluffers can tell their favourite dancers from the stage crew.

GLOSSARY

Characters

A brief run-down of some characters and creatures a bluffer will find in ballet. Anthropomorphism looms large, with only one example of botanomorphism.

Naiads – Water sprites as in *Ondine*.

Dryads – Wood sprites as in *Don Quixote*.

Sylphs – Air sprites as in *La* and *Les*.

Wilis – Girls who die after being jilted before their wedding day. Only recorded sighting is in *Giselle*.

Swans – In the enchanted and dying varieties, with one from Tuonela.

Peri – Guardian of the flowers of immortality and therefore not greatly in demand.

Muses – Mainly ballerinas who inspire, or so it is said, choreographers. As with Fonteyn/Ashton, Seymour/MacMillan, Haydée/Cranko, Farrell/Balanchine. Or when they make a stage appearance, being instructed by Apollo. Terpsichore is the muse of dance.

Nymphs – Winsome goddesses, an obsession of choreographers over the centuries. A case of nymphomania?

Fauns – Half man, half goat, popular in court ballets along with satyrs. Have made only a few afternoon appearances since.

Fairies – In many shapes and sizes in the ballet world; indeed even in some ballets. See *The Dream*, *Cinderella*, etc.

Dolls – Mechanical, or magical, notably *Coppélia, Boutique Fantasque, Nutcracker.*

Birds – As in Blue and Fire, with different species such as cocks, both farmyard and golden. A couple of pigeons make occasional appearances.

Trolls – Gnomic underground beings of gnarled aspect and dreadfully hearty sense of fun, mainly Danish as in *Folk Tale*, with the odd Norwegian, as in *Peer Gynt*.

Butterflies – Not as many as you might imagine, but some in *Piege de Lumière*, *The Concert* and choreographers' stomachs on opening nights.

Friends – Ballerinas invariably appear with a cohort of identikit friends. The ballerina is the one with the fanciest dress.

Whores – Identified by unkempt hair and a bosom-shaking tendency. Seen a lot in MacMillan ballets.

Courtesans – High-class whores of haughty demeanour, in high society or at court. They usually do lots with their fans. Also often seen in MacMillan ballets.

Villagers – Frightfully jolly and healthy young people endlessly folk-dancing, who have obviously managed to avoid the poverty and disease of the period in which their story is set. They live in the tiniest of cottages and make animated conversation about the price of grapes (*Giselle*) or fish (*Napoli*) or the devastating beauty of the ballerina.

Townspeople – As above, but make more sophisticated conversation about the price of whores (*Romeo and Juliet*) and the devastating beauty of the ballerina.

Bayadères – Indian temple dancers with a penchant for penchées. See *La Bayadère*.

Corsaires – Pirates from the north coast of Africa with a penchant for gold lamé trousers.

Danseur noble – A male dancer of the princely type who wouldn't be seen dead appearing as any of the above creatures, but might not object to being a dancing rose.

Poets – Found mooning in the shrubbery suffering from sylphilis as in *Les Sylphides* or having drug-induced fantasies chasing their muse as in Ashton's *Apparitions* or Massine's *Symphonie Fantastique*.

Queen – Often found at the ballet, as well as in them. Degrees of royalty vary from full-blown as in *The Sleeping Beauty* to minor such as the Princess Mother in *Swan Lake*, along with the bad-tempered Queen of the Wilis in *Giselle*.

Ballet Terms

A basic knowledge of ballet technique is essential as no conversation is complete without a sprinkling of technical terms. This is not as daunting as it sounds since you do not actually have to know too much about the steps. (For instance, you can easily learn to recognise the 'Fred step' which is the trademark of Sir Fred's ballets,rather like Alfred Hitchcock's cameo appearances in his own films.) It suffices that certain dancers are particularly remembered for certain things (Darcey's *arabesque*, Johan's *rond de jambe*, etc.) and that the number of basic steps is limited anyway.

Adage – The slow bit which starts a *pas de deux* and is followed by two solos and a coda. Also exercises done in slow tempo.

Allegro – The part of a ballet class made up of fast steps, beats, jumps or turns, and not the only make of car a coryphée can afford.

Arabesque – A pose on one leg with the other leg raised back, the body and arms making a complementary line.

Attitude – Often struck by dancers. Based on the statue of Mercury by Bologna, the dancer stands on one leg with the other raised behind, with the knee bent and the corresponding arm raised.

Ballet blanc – White ballets like *Les Sylphides* or the second act of *Giselle*.

Ballon – Having the attributes of a balloon, in bounce (but not in shape).

Barre – What dancers lean on for support on and off stage.

Battement – Beating movements of the legs performed at the barre.

Batterie – Steps in which the feet beat together or cross when in the air and not the place in which the Golden Cockerel was raised.

Bourrée, pas de – The linking steps performed by the Queen of the Wilis in *Giselle* which make her appear to glide across the stage.

Cabriole – A jumping step in which the dancer raises one leg, bringing the other sharply up to beat with

61

it. Dancers who excel at them can be said to have cabriole legs.

Chat, pas de – Light jumping step, sideways, like a cat.

Coupé jeté – Turning jumps from one foot to the other encircling the stage and nothing to do with fast cars.

Entrechat – The step everyone knows because of its funny name. The dancer jumps in the air and crosses the feet. Be aware that entrechats are numbered, not according to the number of times the feet cross, but the number of changes of position of the feet from ground to ground. An *entrechat dix* has been performed (the feet crossing five times) but it all happens so fast that the dancer looks like a mad gnat in the air. You are not expected to keep count.

Fouetté – The second most famous ballet step in which the ballerina (usually) whips herself into a frenzy of turns. *Fouetté* is French for whip. Get it?

Gargouillade – Not much call for this term, but you might like to know that Dame Marie Rambert called it 'gargling with your feet'. It's like a *pas de chat* with a *rond de jambe* for good measure.

Jeté – Means thrown, but is in fact a jump, though the way some dancers throw themselves into a jump makes it a reasonably accurate term.

Manège – Not a step, but the circular pattern on the stage in which virtuoso jumps are performed.

Pas – As in *de deux*, *de quatre*, means simply, step.

Piqué – Not a mood the ballerina finds herself in, but when she steps directly on to *pointe* without bending the knee or going through the foot – that's **relevé**.

Pirouette – Turn, but not as in 'I've had a nasty turn', though some dancers do have that effect on the audience when they do them.

Plié – From the French for fold. The first exercises at the barre, slowly bending the knees and lowering the body, in the five positions.

Pointe – Standing on the tip of the toe. What ballet is about to most people and what it lacks to others.

Poisson – Fish. A jump with the body arched backwards like a fish jumping out of water is a *temps de poisson*. When the ballerina is caught in this position, as in *Sleeping Beauty*, it is a fish dive or, to be correct, *pas poisson*.

Ports de bras – How dancers carry their arms, not a chest support.

Positions – The five basic turned-out positions of the feet and their related arm movements.

Rond de jambe – The leg is raised with a bent knee. The pointed toe then describes a circle in the air.

Tour en l'air – Mainly performed by men, a jump in the air with a single, double or sometimes triple turn thrown in.

Turn-out – a) the size of the audience; b) the turn-out of the legs from the hips and not, as bluffers should be aware, from the knees or ankles.

THE AUTHOR

Craig Dodd has been involved with the ballet as critic, biographer, sometime agent and general busybody for near 40 years. (He started early.)

Hailing from North Wales where ballet was regarded as a dubious business, he plunged into the ballet world on arrival in the fleshpots of London. His breakthrough into criticism involved writing a piece after a performance and sending it to the now defunct *Ballet Today*. It was published. A similiar ploy worked with *The Guardian* and *The Dancing Times*, a relationship which continues.

His brief experience as agent/manager for many of the stars in this volume confirmed the view that to cope with dancers' egos you have to be a saint or masochist. Or both.

He has written 16 ballet books, total sales of which exceed a million, which you would never tell from his bank balance. For light relief from the serious business of ballet, he operates in the ultimate bluffing business, public relations.

Further titles in the Bluffer's Guide® series:

Accountancy, Archaeology, Astrology & Fortune Telling, Chess, The Classics, Computers, Consultancy, Cricket, Doctoring, The Flight Deck, Football, Golf, The Internet, Jazz, Law, Management, Marketing, Men, Music, Opera, Personal Finance, Philosophy, Public Speaking, The Quantum Universe, Rock Business, Rugby, Science, Secretaries, Seduction, Sex, Skiing, Small Business, Stocks & Shares, Tax, Teaching, University, Whisky, Wine, and Women.

www.bluffers.com